For Fleur Pirotta – SG
For Aunty Ruth & Uncle Peter – SA

Text copyright © 2001 Sam Godwin
Illustrations copyright © 2001 Simone Abel
Volume copyright © 2001 Hodder Wayland

Series concept/design: Dereen Taylor/Liz Black
Book design: Jane Hawkins
Editor: Katie Orchard
Science Consultant: Dr Carol Ballard

Published in Great Britain in 2001 by Hodder Wayland,
an imprint of Hodder Children's Books
This edition reprinted in 2002

A catalogue record for this book is available from
the British Library.

ISBN 07500 3075 5

Printed and bound in Grafiasa, Porto, Portugal

Hodder Children's Books
A division of Hodder Headline Limited
338 Euston Road, London NW1 3BH

From Little Acorns...

A first look at the life cycle of a tree

From Little Acorns...

A first look at the life cycle of a tree

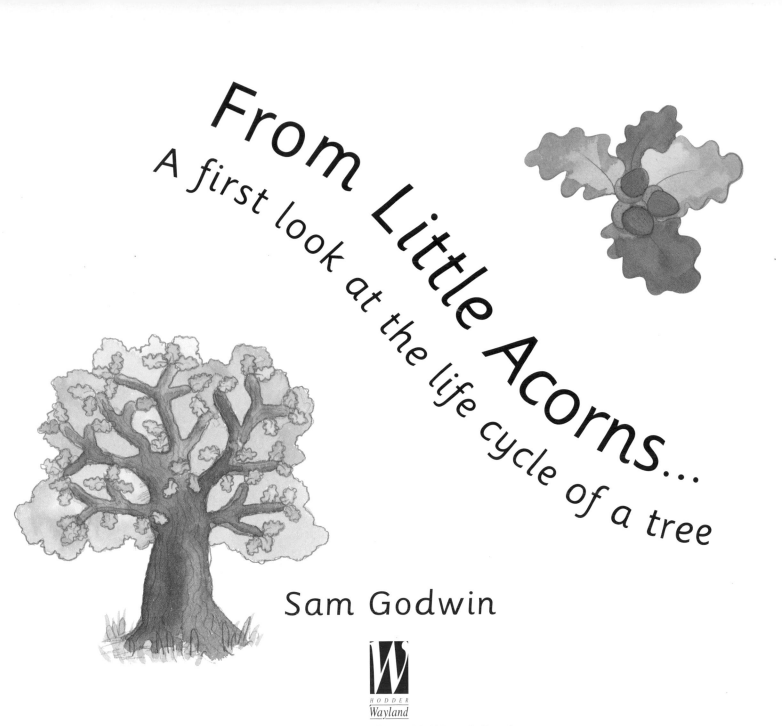

Sam Godwin

HODDER
Wayland

an imprint of Hodder Children's Books

It is autumn. In the wood, acorns

Mummy, something hit me on the head!

BOING!

are falling to the ground.

It's just an acorn. There are lots of them around at this time of year.

Hidden safely under a blanket of leaves,

What's an acorn, Mummy?

8

9

Autumn turns to winter. The acorn lies asleep.

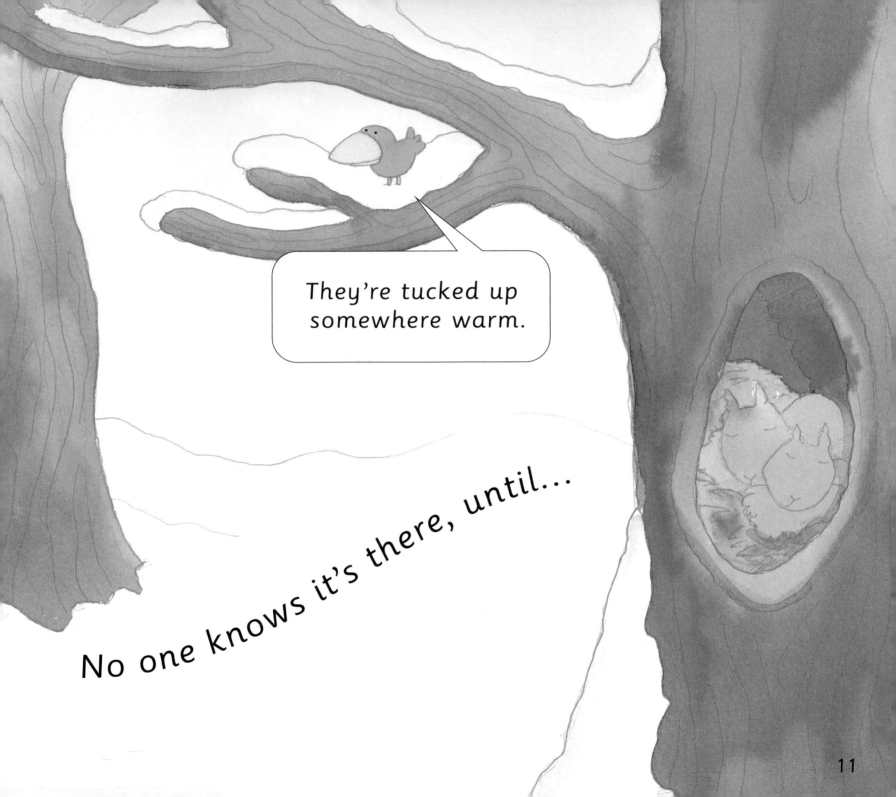

They're tucked up somewhere warm.

No one knows it's there, until...

...spring arrives. The air is warm and damp.

Mummy, has the little acorn grown leaves?

A seedling grows from the acorn.

Yes. Let's hope the caterpillars don't nibble at them.

13

In about three years, the seedling will

grow into a sapling.

This sapling is older than me!

Over thirty years, the branches will get thicker.

That oak tree is 25 metres high!

The sapling will become an oak tree.

Wow! It started as a little acorn.

In summer, flowers appear on the oak tree.

The long flowers are called catkins.

There are small brown flowers, too.

19

As summer turns to autumn,

An oak tree is forty years old when it makes its first acorns.

the small brown flowers become acorns.

Then the acorns fall to the ground.

Most of the acorns are eaten by animals.

But a few survive and grow roots.

With a bit of luck, each acorn will grow up

to be an oak tree.

Some oaks can live for hundreds of years — much longer than us squirrels.

Now that's really old!

27

Yes, we do. We share it with lots of other creatures.

during its lifetime.

Useful words

Acorn
The fruit of an oak tree.

Bark
The rough brown part of a tree trunk.

Catkins
Male flowers, full of pollen.

Roots
The parts of a plant that hold it
in the soil.

Sapling
A young tree. It is too young to make seeds
of its own.

Seed
Part of a flower that will grow into a new plant.

Seedling
A small plant with a green, leafy shoot.

The Oak Tree Life Cycle

1. In late autumn an acorn falls from an adult oak tree. The leaves fall, too.

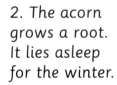

2. The acorn grows a root. It lies asleep for the winter.

3. In spring the seedling grows a shoot with two leaves.

4. The seedling grows more leaves by the end of the summer.

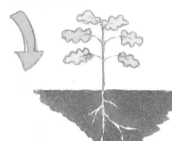

5. After 3 years the seedling becomes a sapling.

6. After 40 years the oak tree is fully grown.

7. In late spring the tree grows flowers.

8. In early autumn there are acorns on the tree.